© 2000 by Barbour Publishing, Inc.

ISBN 1-58660-105-9
ISBN 1-58660-106-7

Selections by Faith Stewart, Patricia Souder, and Viola Ruelke Gommer are used with the authors' permission.

Published by Barbour Publishing, Inc., P.O. Box 719, Uhrichsville, Ohio 44683
http://www.barbourbooks.com

Member of the
Evangelical Christian
Publishers Association

Printed in China.

Good Job!

I'M PROUD OF YOU

written and compiled by
Ellyn Sanna

BARBOUR
PUBLISHING, INC.

You've worked hard to reach this point.
I've watched you grow and learn,
and I've been so proud of you.
You should be proud of yourself as well.
You did a good job!

Contents

Good Job! I'm Proud of You

*Y*ou've accomplished so much these past years.
But this isn't the end—in fact, it's really a whole
   new beginning.
Graduation is the door that opens into adulthood.
This is when you begin to make your own decisions.
This is your time to try your wings and fly.
In the years that come, I pray four things for you:

That you will never underestimate yourself or God.
   Aim high!
That you will be happy. God has so many ways He
   wants to bless you.
That you won't allow discouragement or social pressures
   to stop you. Don't give up!
And that you will always keep your focus clear. Know
   what you want from life—and go for it!

1

Aim High

Those who hope in the LORD. . .
will soar on wings like eagles.

Isaiah 40:31

As you go forward into the years ahead,
  don't be afraid to aim high.
Sometimes it's easier to play it safe and shoot low—
    but if you attempt nothing, you'll never know what
    you could have accomplished.
Dare to try the impossible.
Stand on tiptoe and reach for the stars!
You won't know how high you can go if you
    don't try.

With God all things are possible.

MATTHEW 19:26

*God knows the secret plan
Of the things He will do for the world,
Using your hand.*

Toyohiko Kagawa

Who stops being better stops being good.

Oliver Cromwell

*Do the hardest thing on earth for you.
Act for yourself!
Face the truth.*

Katherine Mansfield

I know sometimes new things can be frightening.
You might feel as though it would be better not to try
    at all than to try and fail.
It's hard to risk falling flat on your face, especially
    if people are watching.
But remember, I believe in you. Take the risk. Push
    your limits.
I know you can do it.

Always be a first-rate version of yourself,
instead of a second-rate version of somebody else.

JUDY GARLAND

I praise you because I am
fearfully and wonderfully made.

PSALM 139:14

Don't look around at what everyone else is doing.
No one is asking you to be someone else.
But the world does need you to be you—
because you are the only one who can do the job.
Be the person God created you to be.
He made you exactly right.

Good Job! I'm Proud of You

You are a part of the great plan, an indispensable part.
You are needed; you have your own unique share
in the freedom of Creation.

MADELEINE L'ENGLE

God saw all
that he had made,
and it was very good.

GENESIS 1:31

Think of it—not one whorled finger exactly like another!
If God should take such delight in designing fingertips, think
how much pleasure the unfurling of your life must give Him.

LUCIE CHRISTOPHER

*I cannot change the whole world,
but I can change a small part of it.*

KAY FLORENTINO

Sometimes you may look around and feel discouraged. After all, you're just one person in an enormous world. But even if you change only one tiny corner for the better, you will have changed the world forever. Even the smallest actions can affect the lives of many; like pebbles tossed in a lake, you never know where the ripples will end.

So don't be afraid to try. Dare to make a difference.

Good Job! I'm Proud of You

Be strong and courageous.
Do not be afraid or terrified. . .
for the LORD your God goes with you;
he will never leave you nor forsake you.

DEUTERONOMY 31:6

) feel that God is calling me to do something
for Him I have not done in the past;
that it is God laying upon me responsibilities
I have not known hitherto;
it is God pointing me to higher heights. . . .

EMMA BOOTH-TUCKER

God is strong. Depending on him alone, I go forward. . . .
O Lord, fill me with the Holy Ghost.
Give me power to move the people.

KIYE SATO YAMAMURO

2

Be Happy

May the God of hope fill you with all joy.

Romans 15:13

Good Job! I'm Proud of You

*Y*ou know how proud I am of you.
I hope you also know how much I want the best
    for you.
No matter where you go, I'll be praying for you,
    asking God to bless you and bring you happiness.
I know sometimes life will seem hard.
I know from time to time you'll feel discouraged
    or confused.
But God doesn't want you to go through life
    feeling sad and dreary.
He wants you to be happy. He wants to give
    you joy.
All you have to do is reach out and take it from
    His hand.

*Y*our success and happiness lie in you. External conditions are the accidents of life, its outer trappings. The great, enduring realities are love and service.

Joy is the holy fire that keeps our purpose warm and our intelligence aglow. Work without joy is nothing. Resolve to keep happy, and your joy and you shall form an invincible host against difficulties.

HELEN KELLER

Good Job! I'm Proud of You

I don't know what your destiny will be, but one thing I know: the only ones among you who will be really happy are those who sought and found how to serve.

DR. ALBERT SCHWEITZER

Your own happiness may seem like a selfish thing to aim for. But really it's not. In fact, it's all wrapped up with other people. You can't be truly happy if you're totally separate from others. And those people who think only of themselves are the most miserable of all.

True happiness is found in giving to others. That's because God created us for relationships. He wants His people to be knit together with love. And loving relationships aren't about taking—they're about giving.

The joy of the LORD is your strength.

NEHEMIAH 8:10

$\int$ ometimes when people graduate, they have trouble going on to the next step. They had so much fun before graduation that they hate to leave it behind. So they're always coming back, always hanging around trying to capture what used to be.

But when you do that, you miss the happiness God has in store for you right here, right now. Make up your mind to enjoy what life offers you in the years ahead.

> *Most people are about as happy as*
> *they make up their minds to be.*

ABRAHAM LINCOLN

Look back—but don't stare. Be happy where you are. Make each day, each stage in your life, your best. This isn't something that just happens if you're lucky. You make this contentment happen. You make the choices. Your life will be what you make it.

And your happiness comes from within you, not from the money you make, the trips you take, or the things you own.

FAITH STEWART

15 Tips for Happiness in Life

- Work at something you enjoy, something that's worthy of your time and talent.

- Have an optimistic attitude. Be positive.

- Forgive others—and yourself.

- Be generous.

- Don't forget to thank God for all His gifts. The more you thank Him, the more gifts you'll notice that He's given you.

- Treat others the way you want to be treated.

- Commit yourself to getting better and better at whatever you do.

- Commit yourself to quality.

- Be a self-starter. Don't wait for someone else to give you a push.

- Find your joy in God and others rather than in possessions.

- Be decisive. Don't be afraid to be wrong. We all make mistakes, but you'll never accomplish anything if you never act at all.

- Give people more than they expect, and give it cheerfully.

- Be generous with your time, your money, your attention. You won't be sorry.

- Don't give up easily. Persist, persist, persist. . .

- Make your Mom proud!

You will rejoice, and no one will take away your joy.

JOHN 16:22

Two people can experience the very same events—and one will respond with sadness and bitterness, while the other finds joy and happiness. Believe it or not, no one can *make* you sad. Of course, sometimes we can't help but be sad when hard things happen. But overall, whether your life is happy or sad depends on your attitude. It's up to you.

So no matter where you go next, no matter what roads life takes you down, my prayer will always be that you will choose to be filled with Christ's joy. Don't let the world's sadness overcome you.

Be happy!

3

Don't Give Up

Be strong in the grace that is in Christ Jesus.

2 TIMOTHY 2:1

We can do anything we want
if we stick to it long enough.

HELEN KELLER

They can conquer
who believe they can.

RALPH WALDO EMERSON

Do a little more each day
than you think you possibly can.

LOWELL THOMAS

$\mathcal{W}$hen I was a kid, I was always starting projects. My shelves were full of half-finished paint-by-number canvas boards, half-done latch-hook rugs, and stories I had begun to write but never finished. Beginning things was always such fun—but sticking with them was harder. Somewhere along the way, I always lost interest. I made mistakes and got discouraged. Or I was just plain bored.

One of the hardest lessons I've had to learn is how to stick with something even when I no longer want to do it, even when it's hard and discouraging, or boring and time-consuming. Giving up is so much easier.

But whether it's a job—or a relationship—I've learned that the rewards of patient endurance will sometimes take you by surprise. So don't give up. My prayer is that you'll have the courage to stick to it. You'll be glad you did!

We do not want you to become lazy,
but to imitate those who through faith
and patience inherit what has been promised.

HEBREWS 6:12

Good Job! I'm Proud of You

The only real failure is to quit.

Anonymous

Success is failure turned inside out—
The silver tint of the cloud of doubt—
And you never can tell how close you are,
It may be near when it seems afar;
So stick to the fight when you're hardest hit—
It's when things seem worst that you must not quit.

George Webster Douglas

Good Job! I'm Proud of You

So do not throw away your confidence;
*   it will be richly rewarded.*
You need to persevere so that
*   when you have done the will of God,*
you will receive what he has promised.

HEBREWS 10:35–36

Oddly enough, God is often the first thing we give up on. We all do it, no matter how "spiritual" we are. One day we're steaming along with God. . .and then little by little, we get distracted or discouraged. After all, we can't see God—but relationships and good times and job responsibilities and even television shows are very visible. It's so much easier to give our attention to the things that are right in front of our eyes. And face it— serving God is just so hard. It goes against our natural selfish tendencies.

God knows how easy it is for us to give up. He understands our human nature. And no matter how many times we give up on Him, He waits patiently, His arms outstretched, for us to turn back to Him.

My prayer for you today, as you graduate, is that you will never stop seeking God's presence. Some days it will be easier than others. But don't give up!

Because God will never give up on you.

*Let us run with perseverance
the race marked out for us.*

HEBREWS 12:1

*Success is to be measured not so much by
the position that one has reached in life as by the
obstacles which he has overcome trying to succeed.*

BOOKER T. WASHINGTON

4

Keep Your Focus

Let us fix our eyes on Jesus,
the author and perfecter of our faith.

HEBREWS 12:2

*R*ight now, on your graduation day, I know you're filled with plans and dreams. Hold on to them. Don't let them slip away.

Life will modify your plans, of course; as you continue to grow and learn, your dreams may change as well. But I believe the basic, central core of who you are today will never change. Be true to that person.

The years ahead will be busy ones. So many new opportunities and responsibilities are coming your way. And that's good. It's wonderful. But don't let yourself be distracted. Keep your focus clear, your vision sharp.

Fix your eyes on Jesus. And everything else will fall into place.

So long as I am acting from duty and conviction,
I am indifferent to taunts and jeers.
I think they will probably do me more good than harm.

WINSTON CHURCHILL

Knowledge is
proud that it knows so much;
wisdom is humble that it knows no more.

WILLIAM COWPER

Without the Way there is no going;
without the Truth there is no knowing;
without the Life there is no living.

THOMAS À KEMPIS

Good Job! I'm Proud of You

*D*on't let the opinions of others distract you from your chosen course. There will always be people who approve of what you are doing—and there will always be those who disapprove. If you let others make up your mind for you, you'll have to do a public opinion poll every time you make a decision. And even then you'll face the disapproval of some.

Listen to the advice of your friends and family. But in the end, remember: It's up to you to decide for yourself. Ask God for His help. He will give you wisdom to know what you should do.

I trust you to hear His voice. You can count on my support.

Trust in the LORD with all your heart
and lean not on your own understanding;
in all your ways acknowledge him,
and he will make your paths straight.

PROVERBS 3:5-6

The Spirit of truth. . .
will guide you into all truth.

JOHN 16:13

The LORD will guide you always;
he will satisfy your needs.

ISAIAH 58:11

*T*hat's not practical."
   "That's silly."
   "That will never work."
   "That's weird."

In the next few years, you'll hear plenty of voices trying to convince you to set another course. But don't listen to those voices, no matter how loud they shout. . .no matter how sweetly they hum in your ear.

Be true to your own vision. Don't let your focus be blurred. I'm counting on you.

This above all:
To thine own self be true:
And it must follow,
as the night the day,
Thou canst not then be
false to any man.

WILLIAM SHAKESPEARE

For the Graduate:

Keeping Your Focus on Your Life's Journey

ratitude is the key to life. It unlocks each day's gifts for you. At the beginning of each day give thanks for all you have experienced.

ead daily. Books open windows into your world. They offer you the gifts of fresh ideas and wisdom for your journey through life.

ccountable—ultimately, you are responsible for the outcomes of your life. Own your actions and decisions.

*D*irected—select a goal and move toward it. Continually evaluate where you are, where you have been, and where you want to go.

*U*nassuming—be aware of your strengths, but know you will also always have areas where you need to grow. Know who you are. Be authentic.

*A*sk. Questions are keys to discoveries. When you show an interest in the world around you, you will find hidden teachers.

*T*ruth—choose the right way, not the wrong way. Be a person of integrity. Seek the truth and it will set you free.

*E*xpect a surprise each day. All things are possible. Expectation brings joy and energy to life.

Good Job! I'm Proud of You

Our Father in Heaven,
   give us the long view of our work and our world.
Help us to see that it is better to fail in a cause that will
   ultimately succeed than to succeed in a cause that
   will ultimately fail. . . .
May Thy will be done here, and may Thy program
   be carried out. . . .
Through Jesus Christ our Lord.
Amen.

PETER MARSHALL

We must believe we are gifted for something,
and that this thing, at whatever cost, must be attained.

MADAME CURIE

Vision without action is a daydream.
Action without vision is a nightmare.

JAPANESE PROVERB

This shall be my parting word:
Know what you want to do—then do it!

ERNESTINE SCHUMANN-HEINK

You have made me so proud. . .
Keep on making me proud!
But more important. . .
Make yourself proud!